TECH GIRLS™

Careers for

TECH GIRLS IN GRAPHIC DESIGN

DONNA B. MCKINNEY

Rosen YA
New York

Published in 2019 by The Rosen Publishing Group, Inc.
29 East 21st Street, New York, NY 10010

Copyright © 2019 by The Rosen Publishing Group, Inc.

First Edition

All rights reserved. No part of this book may be reproduced in any form without permission in writing from the publisher, except by a reviewer.

Library of Congress Cataloging-in-Publication Data

Names: McKinney, Donna Bowen, author.
Title: Careers for tech girls in graphic design / Donna B. McKinney.
Description: New York : Rosen Publishing, 2019. | Series: Tech girls | Includes bibliographical references and index. | Audience: Grades 7–12.
Identifiers: LCCN 2017048545| ISBN 9781508180111 (library bound) | ISBN 9781508180128 (pbk.)
Subjects: LCSH: Commercial art—Vocational guidance—Juvenile literature. | Graphic arts—Vocational guidance—Juvenile literature.
Classification: LCC NC1001 .M35 2018 | DDC 741.6023—dc23
LC record available at https://lccn.loc.gov/2017048545

Manufactured in the United States of America

CONTENTS

INTRODUCTION 4

Chapter **one**

A PERFECT MIX OF TECH AND ART 7

Chapter **two**

GRAPHIC DESIGNERS 16

Chapter **three**

MULTIMEDIA DESIGNERS 24

Chapter **four**

WEBSITE DESIGNERS 33

Chapter **five**

PHOTOGRAPHY 42

Chapter **six**

LANDING THE JOB 49

Chapter **seven**

GRAPHIC DESIGN WRAP-UP 58

GLOSSARY 64
FOR MORE INFORMATION 67
FOR FURTHER READING 70
BIBLIOGRAPHY 72
INDEX 76

Introduction

Many high school girls are intrigued by the idea of a tech career, but they really enjoy art too and don't see how they can pursue both. The great news is that a graphic design career provides the opportunity to work with both art and technology at the same time.

Becca Clason is a graphic designer who combines art and tech as she creates. She is a lettering artist and a stop-motion animator. Much of her design is done working for brands and advertising agencies. Her clients include many well-known names like Starbucks, Target, Disney, Ulta Beauty, and Twitter. Food plays an important role in Clason's creative work. She uses food in unexpected ways to create her lettering and designs.

As a child, Clason enjoyed drawing and painting, so she took art classes. When she entered college, she did not really know anything about graphic design careers, so she chose advertising communications as her major. For that major, she was required to minor in graphic design. The college courses opened her eyes to what a graphic design career involves.

The stop-motion animation part of her career came a little later. In stop-motion animation, a designer takes a photograph of the objects, one frame at a time. Between each photo, the designer moves the objects just slightly, and then takes the

INTRODUCTION

Some young people enjoy the creative freedom of art and the technical capabilities of computers. For them, graphic design could be a great career choice.

next photo. When the images are played back in order, the objects appear to be moving on their own.

Clason started her career working as an advertising art director in New York before shifting to being a full-time freelance graphic designer, living and working in Utah. Interviewed on Design Made Happy, this is Clason's advice to young people considering

5

a career in graphic design: "Don't expect to have a big break or be well-known shortly after graduating from college. I had full-time design jobs for eight years before I had enough freelance business to start doing it full time. I still have a lot to learn as well as improvements I can make."

The graphic design career field, as a whole, is not expected to show a lot of growth in the coming years. The federal Bureau of Labor Statistics (BLS) projected just a 1 percent growth in jobs from 2014 to 2020. But for graphic designers who specialize in working in computer systems design and other related services, BLS anticipates 21 percent growth in jobs during that same time period. Over time, more and more companies are increasing or improving their use of the internet in conducting their business. These companies will need graphic designers skilled at working with website design, so for graphic designers with strong tech skills, the job outlook is encouraging.

The graphic designers of today and tomorrow likely use both a drafting table and a computer, drawing by hand and working at the computer. They will work with a wide range of businesses, from design agencies to advertising agencies to newspapers to book publishers and more. They will be trained in using a variety of computer software programs that provide the technical tools required for design work. And they will have found a way to blend their creative talents and tech skills into a meaningful career.

Chapter one

A PERFECT MIX OF TECH AND ART

Some people enjoy a good art project. They love the creative process. Others like to examine the world, tinkering with the technology that makes things work. What if you are a person who loves to create and has a knack for using technology? For the person who enjoys both the artistic, creative process and the technology that powers our world, graphic design could be just the career. It's the perfect mix of tech and art.

GRAPHIC DESIGN DEFINED

The American Institute of Graphic Arts defines graphic design this way: "Graphic design, also known as communication design, is the art and practice of planning and projecting ideas and experiences with visual and textual content."

Graphic designers use images, words, or graphic forms to create their designs. The finished product of design work can be as tiny as a postage stamp or

CAREERS FOR TECH GIRLS IN GRAPHIC DESIGN

Examples of graphic design work can be seen everywhere. Some of it ends up on large-scale pieces, such as these theater posters.

as huge as signage that covers the side of a building. It might be books, magazines, advertisements, websites, animation, video game graphics, flyers, posters, or billboards. Graphic designers can use technology—computers and computer software—to create their designs. Some graphic designers also work by drawing and creating by hand at a drafting table. And some graphic designers combine the two—drawing by hand and using computer software—to complete their design work.

A PERFECT MIX OF TECH AND ART

POSTAGE STAMP-SIZED DESIGN: GAIL ANDERSON

In Gail Anderson's first attempts at graphic design, she imitated the popular teen magazines she liked to read. Growing up, Anderson says, in an interview for the AIGA Medal, "I used to make little Jackson Five and Partridge Family magazines. I

(continued on the next page)

Gail Anderson (*right*), pictured here with graphic designer Louise Fili, is known for her work with typography. Anderson uses a wide variety of materials to create the type.

9

(continued from the previous page)

wondered who designed *Spec, 16,* and *Tiger Beat* in real life, and as I got older, I began to research what was then called 'commercial art'." She studied at the School of Visual Arts in New York. After completing school, she held jobs at the *Boston Globe Sunday Magazine* and *Rolling Stone*, where she started work as an associate and moved up to become the senior art director. She's an expert on typography, known for creating type using both traditional and unusual materials, such as hot metal, twigs, or bottle caps. After working at *Rolling Stone*, she moved to SpotCo, a large New York City entertainment design agency that creates artwork for plays on and off Broadway. Today she works for the Visual Arts Press at the School of Visual Arts and is also a partner at Anderson Newton Design. In 2008, she received the highest honor given in the graphic design field: the AIGA Medal. Anderson says she is most proud of the "smallest" thing she has ever done—creating the US Postal Service bestselling stamp honoring the 150th anniversary of the Emancipation Proclamation.

Looking beyond graphic designer jobs, there are some other related jobs that might be a good fit for a person interested in art, design, and technology. The federal BLS includes the following in its list of jobs related to graphic design: art directors, craft and fine artists, desktop publishers, drafters, industrial designers, technical writers, and web developers.

HERE'S WHAT IT TAKES

Most graphic design jobs require a bachelor's degree in graphic design or some other related art field. For some entry-level graphic design jobs, a two-year associate's degree or a certificate program might be enough to get a foot in the door working in graphic design.

In the graphic design career field, the person who is hiring is likely going to want to see more than just a college degree when they consider a job candidate. A person seeking a graphic design job will also need to have a portfolio showing examples of their best work. Aspiring graphic designers can build their portfolios through art and design work done in the classroom, through internships, and even through practice, working on their own.

Alongside developing the creative skills for a graphic design career, there is the technology part of the work. Designers still work with pencil, paper, and pens, but these days they also turn to technology tools in many aspects of their work. Computers, design software, tablets, touchpads, and smartphones are part of the graphic designer's technology toolbox.

Sure, it takes an eye for design along with art skills for a career in graphic design. But there are other skills that are important, too. The federal BLS names the following qualities as important for a graphic designer to have: analytical skills, artistic ability, communication skills, computer skills, creativity, and time-management skills. Many of these skills can be sharpened and refined with learning and practice over time. It's not too soon for a student to start honing these qualities and skills while still in school.

START EARLY, START STRONG

If the blend of art and technology that makes up graphic design seems appealing, it is not too early to begin laying the foundation with your high school courses. Take as many of the basic art and design courses available in high school as possible. If your high school offers computer programming courses, these can also help build your foundation, especially if you are interested in web design as a career.

Beyond what is available for high school art classes, there are summer camps and online courses focused on art and design. These camps or online courses can be a good way to gain additional hands-on learning experience and to learn alongside other young people who have similar interests. Many community colleges also offer graphic design courses. Depending on the program, some of these courses might be open to high school students. So it is worth a look to see what is available at any local community college.

Since the requirements for admission vary from school to school, it is smart to be well informed about the requirements for any particular colleges, universities, or art institutes that interest you. As you begin to plan out your high school course schedule, be sure you are taking the courses required for admission to the colleges you might be interested in attending.

In general, students should practice their art and design skills as much as possible. Take time to study art and design in the world around you. If you live close to museums, visit and learn from what is on display there. If museums are far away, the internet is a great tool for observing and learning about design. Take full advantage of your high school years by getting a well-rounded education through studying history, math, science, and the other arts.

GRAPHIC DESIGN GOES TO CAMP

College may still be a few years away, but there is no reason you cannot start learning more about graphic design now. If you live near a community college or university campus, take a look at their summer programs and you might find some summer courses or camps with a graphic design or web design focus. Here is a sample of some graphic design summer camp programs for teens:

- Digital Media Academy—Week-long camps at locations across the country for students ages twelve to seventeen
- New York Film Academy—Teen graphic design camps at US and international locations
- iD Tech Camps—Web design and photography camps for students ages thirteen to seventeen
- Emagination Computer Camps—Game design camp, computer camp, and programming camp for students ages eight to seventeen

CAREERS FOR TECH GIRLS IN GRAPHIC DESIGN

Summer camps and classes can be a great way for young people to improve their graphic design skills in a fun learning environment.

- Syracuse University Summer College for High School Students—Two-week programs with focuses on graphic design, photography, and art
- Watkins College of Art, Design, and Film Pre-College—Two-week intensive summer program for high school students
- Otis College of Art and Design—Summer of Art program for students ages fifteen and up

- UCLA Department of Design Media Arts—Graphic design, web design, audio/video, and gaming for high school students
- American Graphics Institute Summer Program—Web design, web development, graphic design, and video editing for students ages twelve to eighteen

Chapter two

GRAPHIC DESIGNERS

A graphic designer communicates ideas, concepts, and messages using visuals. While text, or words, might be a part of the design, a graphic designer relies heavily on the visual elements of the design to communicate the idea to the people who will be seeing the finished product.

WHAT THEY DO

Although it varies from job to job, a day in the life of a graphic designer might look something like this. The designer is usually working for a client (perhaps some business or organization). The client communicates to the graphic designer the focus, scope, and direction of the project—what the client wants to achieve as the end result.

Based on the client's instructions, the graphic designer works to create a design that tells a certain message or encourages the public to want to buy a certain product. These instructions for the graphic designer might come directly from the client. If the designer is working as part of a larger team, then the instructions might flow from an art director to the graphic design team.

GRAPHIC DESIGNERS

"MASTER CONJURER OF THE INSTANTLY FAMILIAR:" PAULA SCHER

Paula Scher has been at work in the graphic design field for four decades. Since 1991, she's been a partner in the large design studio Pentagram in New York City. Her work is noted for the way it combines pop culture and fine art. As a speaker for TED, Scher is described as the "master conjurer of the instantly familiar." She has done design work for many familiar brands including

(continued on the next page)

Paula Scher brings together the unusual combination of pop culture and fine art in her graphic design work. She is both a teacher and a designer.

17

CAREERS FOR TECH GIRLS IN GRAPHIC DESIGN

(continued from the previous page)

CBS Records, the Public Theater, the Museum of Modern Art, the Metropolitan Opera, New York City Ballet, and Microsoft. In 2001, she received the highest honor given in the graphic design field, the AIGA Medal. In 2006, she became the first woman to win the Type Directors Club Medal. In addition to her work as a designer, Scher is also helping to train the next generation of graphic designers, teaching at the School of Visual Arts in New York, Cooper Union, Yale University, and the Tyler School of Art. Her work is part of permanent collections at the Museum of Modern Art, Cooper-Hewitt National Design Museum, and the Library of Congress, to name just a few.

The graphic designer works by hand or using computer software (or with a combination of both) to create the desired images. The designer makes decisions—colors, layouts, images, and typefaces—to communicate the client's desired message. Once the designer completes the image, the client (or the art director) reviews the work and makes suggestions or changes before the designer reworks and fine-tunes it into a completed, final image. This final product might be used as a printed page (for example, as part of a book, magazine, poster, chart, product, or illustration) or as part of a website or video game.

Graphic designers need to be good at multitasking. They are often required to work on more than one project at a time and expected to shift gears quickly in moving between their work on the various projects. Some designers may specialize in one kind of work, such as multimedia, websites, photography, or videography, but the kind of work needed will depend on the graphic design job.

WHERE THEY WORK

A graphic designer usually works in a full-time position for a company. Many designers work for design or advertising agencies. In these jobs, the designer usually works on projects coming from a variety of outside clients. Jobs with an advertising firm can be a great starting point for new graphic designers who are just coming into the workforce after college. Because of the nature of advertising work, graphic designers usually get the chance to work with both print and digital ads, along with other types of products. These jobs offer young graphic designers the opportunity to sharpen their skills in a wide variety of projects.

Some graphic designers find jobs working in-house for a large organization or company. In this type of role, the designer usually works on a wide variety of products covering all of the company's creative design needs. The graphic designers who work in-house for a specific company get the opportunity to work on a single brand and really see the development of that brand over time. A junior graphic designer is usually working with and learning from a senior designer or a team of designers.

CAREERS FOR TECH GIRLS IN GRAPHIC DESIGN

Graphic designers who land jobs with big organizations or companies usually work on a wide range of creative products. They are often part of a larger design team.

Looking ahead in a graphic designer's career path, someone who has several years of experience working as a designer might be ready to apply for supervisory jobs, such as art director or creative director. In these director positions a designer usually has more responsibility for the overall project design and then directs the designers and others who create the artwork.

Some graphic designers choose to work as freelancers instead of working in-house for a

FINDING THE RIGHT SCHOOL

If you have decided that you want to pursue a career in graphic design, then one of your next steps might be searching for the schools that offer the training you need. There are tools that can help you in your search for the right school. As you think about colleges, take a look at the National Association of Schools of Art and Design (NASAD) website. They have a searchable online listing of "accredited institutions." The list of about 360 schools includes colleges, universities, and institutes that provide training in art and design. This NASAD list (https://nasad.arts-accredit.org) could be a very helpful tool as you begin to think about college. Your high school guidance counselor might be another helpful resource as you begin to research colleges.

company. Like some of the other creative-type jobs such as writers or artists, graphic designers can also be self-employed. The work of a graphic designer can lend itself to a freelance or part-time schedule. The federal BLS reported in 2014 that about one in five graphic designers were self-employed.

Working as a freelance graphic designer means a person has a flexible schedule and freedom in choosing work projects, and this is very appealing to some people. But the freelancer also has to do the work of finding and bidding on jobs. These graphic designers also need to have a working knowledge of the business side of things. Filing taxes, tracking work hours, purchasing insurance, and billing are necessary business skills for the self-employed or freelance designer. Where designers working for a design or ad agency, or a large company, draw a regular paycheck, freelancers have to learn to live with a not-so-steady flow of income.

GET READY

For the high school student trying to decide the path to take to gain a graphic design education, there are several choices. If you're trying to decide between a two-year associate's degree or a four-year bachelor's degree, here are some things to consider:

In the two-year program, there is usually more emphasis on technical skills. Community college programs in graphic arts are readily available. At some schools, you might see a little variation in the program names, for example, it might be named digital arts, advertising and graphic design, computer graphics, or integrated media. These schools usually offer a two-year associate's degree or a certificate program.

In a four-year program, students usually complete the liberal arts course requirements needed for the bachelor's degree. While a two-year degree may be enough to qualify you for some graphic design positions, there will be many jobs where a four-year degree is a mandatory requirement for you to even be considered for a position. To start your search for a school, the National Association of Schools

GRAPHIC DESIGNERS

Graphic design courses and degree programs can be found at both community colleges and four-year colleges and universities.

of Art and Design provides a listing of accredited institutions on its website. Talk to your art teacher (or someone you know who works in graphic design) and ask about where he or she attended school and the kind of training he or she got.

Graphic designers also need to be proficient in using computer design software programs. You can learn these software programs working on your own or by taking formal courses.

23

Chapter three

MULTIMEDIA DESIGNERS

Some graphic designers specialize and work in multimedia design as artists or animators. They create the images and special effects that entertain people through websites, television, movies, video games, and other kinds of interactive applications. A multimedia designer uses more than one medium to communicate an idea to the audience. Where a graphic designer usually works with images (just one format) that communicate an idea, a multimedia designer might combine images and sound (two or more formats) to convey an idea.

WHAT THEY DO

Multimedia design jobs involve creating the audio, animation, and graphics for television, movies, video games, learning software, websites, and other media. They combine text, images, video, and audio to entertain or to communicate a message or idea to the audience. The animator or artist usually works as part of a team.

The multimedia artists or animators create the computer-generated imagery (CGI) or 3D animations used in television, video games, or movies. These designers can create characters, locations, objects, and special effects using computer hardware and software. Examples of CGI are found in movies like *Star Wars, Episode* 1 (1999), *The Matrix* (1999), *Avatar* (2009), *Transformers: Dark of the Moon* (2011), and *The Jungle Book* (2016).

Even the annual Emmy awards, recognizing excellence in the television industry, honor a multimedia designer. There is an Emmy award given at the ceremony to the television program with "Outstanding Main Title Design." The main title is that short video shown at the beginning of a television show. Sometimes it is called the "opening credits," and it is usually thirty to sixty seconds long. Typically, this award is given each year to the multimedia designer who created the best main title for that year.

Besides working with film, television, or video games, multimedia designers can find jobs in the field of education, creating instructional materials that combine sound and images to provide interactive teaching products.

Artists and animators can work in different ways. Some create their designs, working with computer software or even by writing their own computer code. Other artists and animators may choose to draw or paint by hand first and then rework their images using computer programs later.

Some artists and animators use storyboards as a way of organizing their animation work. In storyboarding, the artist or animator brings together the elements—images, text, video, and audio—in a

CAREERS FOR TECH GIRLS IN GRAPHIC DESIGN

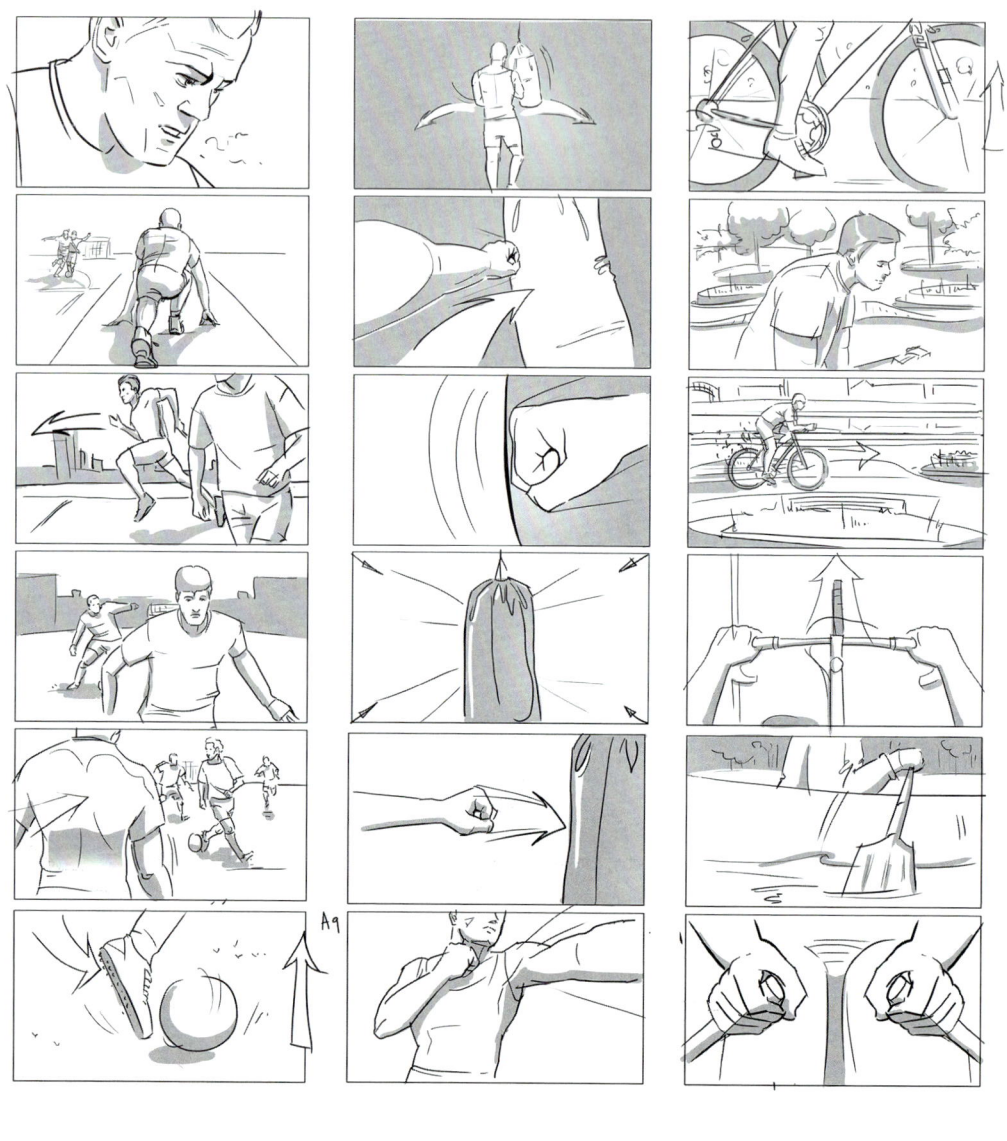

Graphic designers sometimes use storyboards for animation work. These sketches tell the story in comic strip format and show how the work might appear in its finished form.

step-by-step sequence of individual drawings. Put together, these individual drawings are like a comic strip that tells the story. The storyboard allows the artist and other members of the creative team to visualize how the movie, animation, or game might appear in its final form.

Even in the field of multimedia design, some artists and animators become specialists. For example, an artist might specialize in creating just the characters or just the scenery and background design in animated movies and video games. Some may focus their work on creating the layouts for the different levels of a video game.

WHERE THEY WORK

Many multimedia designers work in the entertainment industry—creating the movies, television, and video games that people enjoy watching and playing. However, there are some designers who work as in-house designers, creating visuals and multimedia presentations for corporations and organizations.

Like other graphic designers, some multimedia designers choose to work as freelancers too. The federal BLS reports that about half of the multimedia artists and animators in the United States are self-employed. Most of the other animators and artists are employed at companies connected to the movie and video industries. The BLS reports that the median annual salary for multimedia artists and animators is higher than the salary for general graphic designers.

CAREERS FOR TECH GIRLS IN GRAPHIC DESIGN

ERGONOMICS

Ergonomics is the science of making things for the workplace that are both comfortable, safe, and efficient. Once upon a time, graphic designers might have been happy with a drafting table, a well-lit room, and a sturdy chair. Because of the study of ergonomics, today's graphic designers have many options when it comes to outfitting their work space. Most people agree that sitting at a desk all day is not good for a person's health. As an

For the graphic designer who tires of sitting all day, working at a standing desk or even a treadmill desk, as pictured here, is an option.

alternative, some graphic designers work at standing desks or variable desks (which can be easily changed from the sitting to standing position). And for the more energetic graphic designers, there are treadmill desks, where a person can exercise while working. Ergonomic chairs and stools are also available, specially designed to prevent the kind of back pain that comes from long stretches of sitting. The computer keyboard, mouse, and mouse pad are designed with ergonomic features now, too.

Multimedia designers usually follow a regular work schedule, but when working on projects with approaching deadlines, evening or weekend work hours might be necessary.

GET READY

Multimedia artists and animators can find associate's degree programs in multimedia education. These associate-level programs usually teach a more hands-on approach, focusing on the tools and techniques needed for multimedia design jobs. But when multimedia artists and animators go looking for jobs, they will find that most employers are seeking someone with a bachelor's degree.

A major in fine art, computer graphics, animation, multimedia design, multimedia studies, or some other related field would be a good fit for people seeking multimedia artist or animator jobs. (A computer graphics major usually adds in some computer

CAREERS FOR TECH GIRLS IN GRAPHIC DESIGN

Multimedia design work calls for strong technical skills. Keeping up with the ever-changing technology through courses or on-the-job training is a must.

science courses along with the art courses.) In addition to a bachelor's degree, potential employers will also want to see a portfolio of work that demonstrates strong technical skills and know-how.

Multimedia designers generally are familiar with using the Adobe Creative Suite (now called the

Adobe Creative Cloud), a software suite consisting of applications such as Photoshop, Acrobat, Illustrator, InDesign, After Effects, Flash, and Premiere Pro. Animation studios that use their own software and applications to make their movies will normally provide training for anyone they hire.

The BLS projected that jobs for multimedia artists and animators will increase 6 percent between 2014 and 2024. Consumer demand for bigger, better, more eye-popping visual effects in movies, video games, and television will help feed the need for more animators and artists. One specific area of growth will be the need for multimedia designers who can create the computer graphics required for use on smartphones.

DO-IT-YOURSELF: GRAPHIC DESIGN ONLINE

Maybe attending a summer camp program for art, design, or technology does not fit into your schedule or your budget. Maybe your high school offers only one basic art course. Do not let these obstacles discourage you as you pursue the dream of being a graphic designer. You can still strengthen your art and design skills through some of the online courses available. An internet search of "graphic design online courses for teens" can help you find the available courses. Here are just a few of the options:

- Digital Media Academy—Courses for students aged ten and older in graphic design, game design, and programming
- TechRocket—Courses for students from ages ten to eighteen in graphic design, coding, and game design
- Youth Digital—Courses for students aged eight to fourteen in coding, design, and animation

Chapter four

WEBSITE DESIGNERS

Some graphic designers specialize in website design. A web designer (or website designer) creates the look and feel of websites and other related applications.

WHAT THEY DO

The web designer's job involves working with color, images, typography, and layout to create the website. In addition to having graphic design skills, it can be very useful for a web designer to also be proficient working with computer languages such as HTML, CSS, and JavaScript. With the constantly changing technology, skilled web designers study and practice to keep pace with the technology needed for their work.

For the user looking at a webpage, it can be easy to overlook all the work that goes on behind the scenes to create a page that is both easy to use and visually appealing. It is the web designer's job to build that easy-to-use, beautiful website. It calls for a combination of strong design skills and strong technical skills.

CAREERS FOR TECH GIRLS IN GRAPHIC DESIGN

The designer must consider the "audience"—who will be using the website—when working to create webpages that can meet the user's needs. This involves a designer who is listening carefully

A web wireframe, pictured here, is like a blueprint for a website. Designers use a wireframe to help organize the elements of a website.

and asking smart questions to better understand the client's needs. For example, the colors, fonts, and layout a designer chooses might be different for a younger audience compared with an older audience. A website designed for children would look very different from a website designed for professional employees, such as doctors, lawyers, or engineers. Learning about the intended audience and then creating a website to meet that audience's needs is the designer's goal.

The job titles "web designer" and "web developer" sound similar, and there is some overlap in the two jobs. Simply described, the difference between the two is that designers handle the design part of the work and developers handle the coding. Designers are focused on the beauty or visual appeal and the usability of the website. Their goal is to make the website both appealing to the eyes and easy to navigate. Developers use the technology to bring to life the design work done by the designer.

While these jobs exist as separate positions, there are some people who have skills in both design and development—they can be hired for hybrid-type positions called web designer/developer.

WHERE THEY WORK

Web designers can find work in many different kinds of businesses. There is a need for web designers in creative businesses, like design agencies, and also in industries that conduct their business on the web. More and more companies—from doctor's offices to grocery stores to hair salons—need a web presence, as more and more people turn to the web to do business and find information. These companies need the services of web designers to

SHE ENJOYS THE COLLABORATION: JESSICA WALSH

Jessica Walsh is a graphic designer and art director for the design agency Sagmeister & Walsh in New York City. She got a very early start in her career—she was coding and designing websites when she was just eleven years old. Walsh did freelance website work for people and small businesses during her high school years. She even created an HTML website that provided free graphic templates for other young people to use. That website provided her with some income through its advertising, and Walsh began to realize that she might be able to turn her passion for design into a job someday. Today her clients include Jay-Z, the *New York Times*, Levi's, and the Museum of Modern Art, to name just a few. *Forbes* magazine named her on its list of "30 under 30 top creatives designing the future." Walsh says in an interview with designboom, "I prefer working on a team versus solo, I think a collaborative effort between creatives with different kinds of skills yields more interesting results than one person could do alone." When asked what she knows now that she wishes she had known when she was twenty-one, Walsh replied, "Doing great work is not enough. When I was younger, I didn't used to appreciate the amount of energy that goes into finding/getting the right clients and selling your ideas through to clients."

keep themselves competitive in the marketplace. Many companies who already have web pages need to be sure their websites are accessible from mobile devices and tablets.

As with other kinds of graphic design jobs, web designers can also work on a freelance basis for a number of clients, based in a home office. Freelancing gives people the freedom to choose their clients and shape their own work hours. But a freelancer also has to handle the business aspects of

For some freelancers, "going to work" might mean just sitting down in a home office. Graphic design work can easily be done from home.

CAREERS FOR TECH GIRLS IN GRAPHIC DESIGN

the job, such as finding clients, filing taxes, or billing hours. A web designer considering freelance work over a staff position working for a company should carefully consider the pros and cons before deciding.

Web design jobs, whether freelance or staff positions, easily lend themselves to remote work—where members of the design team can be working from their home offices in different locations.

DESIGN ON DISPLAY AT THE MUSEUM

Sometimes people think of art museums as places that house the work of artists from long ago. But did you know that digitally designed works from the present day are finding their way into art museums, too? If you are fortunate to live close to an art museum, plan a visit and check out its design collection. If an in-person visit is not possible, you still might enjoy viewing the museums' web page. Here are some well-known museums with digital design collections:

- Victoria and Albert (V&A) Museum, London, United Kingdom (https://www.vam.ac.uk)
- Museum of Modern Art (MoMA), New York, New York (https://www.moma.org)
- Cooper Hewitt, Smithsonian Design Museum, New York, New York (https://www.cooperhewitt.org)
- San Francisco Museum of Modern Art (SFMOMA), San Francisco, California (https://www.sfmoma.org)
- Design Exchange (DX), Toronto, Canada (http://www.dx.org)

WEBSITE DESIGNERS

The work of graphic designers is now finding a home in art museums. Next time you visit an art museum, ask if there is digital design work on display.

- Museum of Design Atlanta (MODA), Atlanta, Georgia (http://www.museumofdesign.org)
- Chicago Design Museum (ChiDM), Chicago, Illinois (https://chidm.com)

GET READY

Web designers should plan to have at least an associate's degree, and a bachelor's degree is preferred. A major in graphic design, website design, computer science, or computer technology helps to prepare you for a web designer job. Some schools might offer a degree in graphic arts with a concentration in web design. Even within the field of web design, some people might specialize, for example, pursuing training in website programming or internet marketing.

Knowledge of programming languages such as HTML, CSS, and JavaScript is useful for the web designer. Designers also use graphic design software,

Some graphic designers find that knowledge of computer programming languages is a great asset in their work. Having some programming skills enhances their design abilities.

such as Photoshop, Illustrator, Dreamweaver, Inkscape, and GIMP. Knowing how to work with various media programs in order to add sound or film clips to web pages is also a useful part of the designer's skill set.

Some web designers write the copy for the client's pages, so strong writing skills can definitely be an asset for a designer. In other cases, the clients provide the copy, and the web designer simply works with that copy in building the web pages.

In addition to pursuing formal training or education, a person seeking a web design job will need to have a strong digital portfolio (sometimes called an electronic portfolio or an e-portfolio). This portfolio is usually maintained on the web and provides examples of a person's best design work.

A good first step to gaining practical experience as a web designer is to build a site. Some designers get their start by volunteering to create a website for a nonprofit or a community group. Others may have some special interest or hobby, and they build a website around that interest. Don't be afraid to do some unpaid work if it might help get you noticed in positive ways once you begin your actual job hunt.

Chapter five

PHOTOGRAPHY

Some graphic designers choose to use photography as a part of their design work. Other designers with photographic skills might offer their clients services in both design and photography. Some companies advertise jobs seeking a person who has both graphic design and photography skills. Designers might look to photographs for inspiration and ideas as part of their design work process. And some designers might simply enjoy photography as a hobby. Whether or not graphic designers pursue formal training in photography, having these skills can benefit them in a variety of ways in their general design work.

PHOTOGRAPHY TOOLS

Graphic designers who choose to take their own photos for their design work need the combination of an artistic eye and strong technical skills to operate the high-end camera equipment available today. Digital cameras are the work tool for many designers shooting photographs these days, instead of traditional film cameras. Graphic designers who want to improve their photography skills do not have to sink a lot of money into buying a fancy, expensive camera. (Camera gear can be very pricey.) And having an expensive camera does not guarantee that you will be able to shoot fantastic photographs. Starting out with a less expensive camera and learning basic photography skills can be a smart path toward becoming a better photographer.

Using a digital camera, designers can store their electronic images on disks, cards, or flash drives. Then, back at their computers, they can edit and enhance their photos with the wide range of photo editing software that is available. The photo editing software available today gives designers the powerful tools needed to manipulate or enhance images in many different ways. Designers have a number of photo editing software programs to choose from, such as Adobe Photoshop, Serif PhotoPlus, Corel Paintshop, or CyberLink PhotoDirector, to name just a few. These photo editing software programs can be complex to learn, so spending some money on a formal class (instead of just learning on your own) can be a smart investment.

A CAREER OF "FIRSTS": CIPE PINELES

Cipe Pineles (1908–1991) was born in Austria and came to live in the United States when she was a teenager. At that time, the fields of art and design were mainly a man's world. Pineles stepped into that man's world with several important firsts. When

(continued on the next page)

(continued from the previous page)

she was searching for her first graphic design job in the 1940s, some employers saw her portfolio and were interested in her work until they realized that "Cipe" was the name of a woman. She persisted in her pursuit of a job and eventually landed a position as art director for *Glamour* magazine in 1942. Pineles was the first woman to hold that position at a major American magazine. She went on to work as art director at *Seventeen* magazine and *Charm* magazine. Pineles used specialists in fine art to do the illustrating work in the mass-market magazines where she was art director—an inventive move for the day. This practice brought young magazine readers into contact with fine art and gave fine artists a path into the commercial world of magazines. Pineles also taught at the Parsons School of Art and Design. She became the first woman inducted as a member of the New York Art Directors Club in 1948. Her career spanned almost sixty years, until her death in 1991.

Cipe Pineles was truly a pioneer in graphic design. She was the first woman in many of the jobs she held, opening doors for other female designers.

PHOTOGRAPHY IN DESIGN WORK

Graphic designers who add some photography skills to their toolbox of experience might notice several advantages as they do their design work. A designer who also shoots photos develops a sharper eye for things like layout, composition, color, balance, and contrast. These are important in both graphic design

To achieve that "just right" photograph for a certain project, a designer may have to travel to interesting places or work with unusual materials.

and photographic work. Designers with photography skills also develop an eye for seeing the "story" that the image is telling.

Some designers use stock photos in their work. These are photos that are sold or licensed for use. This process gives graphic designers quick and easy access to the photos they need for their projects. Having some photography experience can be useful for designers when searching for and identifying stock photos they need for their work.

When designers work with stock photos, they do not have the same control over the images as they do if they shoot their own custom images themselves. For this reason, some designers prefer to shoot their own photos. A graphic designer who uses stock photos may have to settle for an image that is almost but not quite right for the design idea they have in mind. By shooting their own photographs, designers can create that "just-right" image for their design work.

ADDING THE PHOTOGRAPHY SKILLS

Graphic designers who want to strengthen their photography skills may accomplish this in several ways. If you are pursuing a graphic design degree in college, you may find that photography or photojournalism are available as course selections. Taking a college course or two in photography is one way to gain these skills. Some schools combine graphic design and photography into one program, so a student could pursue one curriculum focusing on both design and photography.

A DESIGNER WHO TEACHES THE NEXT GENERATION: ALLISON BLAYLOCK

Allison Blaylock teaches graphic design to high school students in the Charlotte, North Carolina, area. She's also a graphic designer working part-time for a church, where she handles design needs for a wide range of ages and programs. She thinks she has the best of both worlds—getting to do her own design work and sharing her knowledge and skills with the next generation. Blaylock remembers enjoying art projects as a child. In high school, she took a lot of art classes. And she says she was fortunate to have teachers who pushed her to get her work out into the community at festivals and competitions. Even while in high school, she began to get commissions for her paintings and design work. After high school, Blaylock attended Appalachian State University where she earned two degrees—a bachelor of fine arts in photography and sculpture and a bachelor of science in art education. Her college professors told her, "you're already good at painting, so try something else." That push toward something new led her to graphic design. She started doing digital media and found she really enjoyed it, so she took more of those classes for her photography degree. This is Blaylock's advice for young people interested in graphic design: "You have to try everything and then you'll find something that is your niche." She also encourages high school students to find ways to do design work, even on a volunteer basis; you can design a set of business cards for a friend or create a poster for a neighborhood event to gain experience. Her last word of advice: "Just because you have one failure doesn't mean you're not a success somewhere else." Keep trying!

When looking for a summer job or internship, you may want to consider working as an assistant to a professional photographer in a sort of apprentice role. This can be an excellent way to gain hands-on experience.

Young people can begin getting photography experience by taking any available photography classes in high school or enrolling in summer camps or classes that have a photography focus. A photography job for the high school newspaper is another great way to gain experience.

Chapter six

LANDING THE JOB

Most people do not just stumble into jobs without planning or thought. Usually some work is required. Even as a student still in school, you can start thinking about career opportunities and lay the foundation for future jobs. Whether it is part-time jobs or internships that you want now or a full-time job that you would like to have later, you can begin the work of preparing yourself for the job hunt.

BUILDING A DIGITAL PORTFOLIO

There's a familiar saying, "a picture is worth a thousand words." When you are looking for a job in the graphic design field, the "pictures," or images and designs, truly do speak for themselves. You are going to need to be able to showcase examples of your work in the best way possible. Creating a digital portfolio is a great way to display your work for any prospective employer or as you apply to colleges.

For example, the Pratt Institute, one of many good design schools in the United States, gives this advice to students preparing their portfolios: "Is the work you are submitting telling us about who you are, what you've been doing, what your opinion is, where you want to go? … Use your creativity and skills to address these questions visually. We want to see that

CAREERS FOR TECH GIRLS IN GRAPHIC DESIGN

you are willing to take some risks, go beyond what is asked of you, and that you are asking big questions." You want to build a digital portfolio that truly shines as a reflection of your best work.

This digital portfolio is a computer-based collection of a student's best work. It is usually assembled and kept on the web. The portfolio likely changes over time as a student learns new skills or attempts new types of design work and adds these new samples of work to the portfolio. An internet

With a digital portfolio, graphic designers showcase samples of their best work. Even before getting a job, students can start building a portfolio of work.

50

search of "how to create a digital portfolio" will provide lots of examples and how-tos for building the portfolio. (Sometimes it is called an electronic portfolio, e-portfolio, or online portfolio—just slightly different names for the same thing.)

The digital portfolio is usually arranged in sections, such as homepage, about me, selected works, and résumé. There are web applications that help you build the online portfolio without having to know web development coding. These web apps include Crevado, Behance, Carbonmade, Morpholio, Squarespace, and Viewbook, to name just a few.

WRITING A RÉSUMÉ AND COVER LETTER

Writing a résumé, especially that first résumé, may be a challenge. You may wonder, what I am going to put in my resume if I've never had a real job? That is a good question. But even students just entering the workforce for the first time can craft a résumé that helps to showcase their skills in the best possible way.

A résumé usually lists your contact information (name, address, email address, phone number), education, experience, activities, and awards. An internet search for "high school résumés" will provide plenty of sample résumés and even templates so you can see some different ways of building your résumé.

CAREERS FOR TECH GIRLS IN GRAPHIC DESIGN

GRAPHIC DESIGN CONFERENCES: BE A LIFELONG LEARNER

Even after you have landed that graphic design job, it is important to stay tuned in to new developments in the field. Commit to being a lifelong learner. One way to keep your knowledge and skills strong is to attend graphic design conferences. Here are just a few of the many graphic design conferences available each year:

The learning doesn't end with a college diploma. Going to design conferences is one way graphic designers can keep up with the latest in design and technology.

52

LANDING THE JOB

- HOW Design Live—This conference describes itself as "one of the largest annual gatherings of creative professionals in the world."
- AIGA Design Conference—An annual conference hosted by AIGA, the professional association for design.
- Adobe MAX: The Creativity Conference—This conference describes itself as the "perfect blend of ... practical knowledge and creative magic."

Don't worry that your "experience" is very limited. Maybe you have not yet had a paying job. But experience can also include volunteer opportunities. Think about any volunteer experience you might have gained through school, community organizations, or a church group. Also think of chores you might do for neighbors and relatives as experience. Jobs like babysitting, dog walking, or yard chores count as experience also.

A cover letter accompanies the résumé that you send out to the person or company that is hiring. Think of the cover letter as a formal way of introducing yourself to the person making the job hiring decisions. Just as with the résumé, if you do an internet search for "cover letters" you can find plenty of helpful examples.

Often your résumé and cover letter are going to make the first impression, even before the person doing the hiring has a chance to meet you. So be sure they make a great first impression. Before you send that résumé and cover letter anywhere, read them carefully to catch any punctuation or spelling mistakes. Then read them again. It is always hard to proofread your own work, so get a second opinion. Ask an adult to proofread your cover letter and résumé, too.

NETWORKING TIPS

Networking just means getting to know people. In the job-hunting world, it is getting to know people who can help you find opportunities for work. Your network might include classmates, teachers, coaches, counselors, or your parents's friends—anynoe who might have information about a new job or who might know someone who could help you in your job search.

Wherever you meet people—at school, the library, church—listen carefully and consider whether the person might be able to help you in your job search. Introduce yourself and ask questions. If the thought of speaking to someone you do not know makes you nervous (and even many adults get nervous in these situations), then practice introducing yourself. Jot down a list of things you would want to say when introducing yourself to someone who might help you land a job—such as your name, your school, and what you are interested in doing—and then run through your intro while you are alone at home. You will feel more confident when meeting new people.

Social media can be a helpful tool in networking. Use it to connect with businesses, people who are

LANDING THE JOB

WHO'S THE BOSS? WOMEN-OWNED GRAPHIC DESIGN COMPANIES

Some graphic designers start their own companies, managing both the business and creative sides of the work. Take a look at a few of these women-owned graphic design companies:
- Clean Design—Owned by Natalie Perkins in Raleigh, North Carolina
- Willoughby Design—Founded by Ann Willoughby in Kansas City, Missouri, and San Francisco, California
- Oblique Design—Owned by Janice Ferrante in Boulder, Colorado
- Marquis Design—Owned by Julie Vail in Boston, Massachusetts
- KTD Creative—Founded by Kate Tallent in Washington, DC
- Tall Girl Design—Founded by Pam Perkins and Debbie Oberg in Orchard Park, New York

hiring, colleges, and other teens interested in graphic design. Older teens can create a LinkedIn profile and use it to display their résumés and samples of their work.

If your work experience is very limited (or even nonexistent) then you might find that looking for an unpaid internship is a smart first step. Look at it as a valuable learning experience that will be very beneficial when you go looking for a paying job a few years later.

CAREERS FOR TECH GIRLS IN GRAPHIC DESIGN

NAILING THE JOB INTERVIEW

In most cases, the prospective employer will be meeting you for the first time when you walk through the door for the interview. Try your best to be prepared for the interview opportunity.

PUT YOUR BEST FOOT FORWARD

You'll want to make the best first impression possible. Arrive a few minutes early. Dress neatly. Silence your phone and put it away during the interview. Look at the person you are talking to and shake the person's hand when you arrive.

"You've got the job!" Walk into a job interview confident and prepared. It's an important first step toward getting that design job you want.

BE PREPARED

Bring several copies of your résumé and also a notepad (you might want to write down the interviewer's name, so you have it in front of you, or jot down any questions you might have). Bring your portfolio (paper copies of your best work, even if you also have a digital portfolio), so that if the person hiring wants to talk about your work samples, you will have them close at hand.

    It is normal to feel nervous, but try to be positive and enthusiastic while you are in the interview. Spend some time before the interview thinking about your strengths—the things you do well. Interviewers often ask people they interview to describe their strengths. So think and be ready to talk about your attitudes and activities that would help to make you a great employee. Also, do some research about the company you are interviewing with so you are prepared. Spend some time on the company's website, learning about what they do and how they do it. Don't be afraid to ask questions.

SAY THANKS

Once you have left the interview, write a short thank-you note or email, thanking the interviewer for taking time to talk with you and letting the person know you are interested in the job (if you are).

Chapter seven

GRAPHIC DESIGN WRAP-UP

Maybe you knew you wanted to pursue a career using your artistic skills back in elementary school when you spent more time designing your book report covers than you did writing the book report. Or perhaps you look at a sign and the first thing you notice is the fonts chosen for the lettering. Maybe you've always loved every single one of the sixty-four colors in your crayon box. Graphic design can be a great career because it allows you to explore your creative side while staying up to date and skilled in the latest design software available.

LOOK AT THE ADVANTAGES

The advantages of a graphic design career are plentiful. You get to be creative—every day you get to apply your imagination and skills to being the most creative person you can be … and someone pays you to do it. You also get to work alongside other creative people because a fair amount of design work is done in teams.

There's flexibility in a graphic design career. Some people choose to work for a design agency or advertising agency. Others pursue jobs as in-house designers working for a company or the government. And still others choose to be self-employed, working as freelance designers. Both working for someone else and working as a freelancer have their pros and cons. The good thing is that the graphic design field allows you to choose the working style you prefer.

KEEP ON LEARNING

There are other ways a graphic design career offers flexibility. A designer can choose whether to work on the web or with print materials. Think of the other choices a designer has: books, magazines, ads, websites, video games, animation, posters, or signs, to name just a few.

Another advantage of being a graphic designer is that you get to be a lifelong learner. It seems there is always new technology rolling out in the marketplace, whether it be computers, cameras, printers, or new design software. A graphic designer cannot sit on the sidelines ignoring new technology. Technology is such an integral part of creative work that graphic designers must invest time in learning to use it in order to keep pace.

TAKE A LOOK AT THE BLOGS

You can find blogs to see examples of famous (or not-so-famous) designers's work. To get started, do an internet search for "graphic design blogs"—there are many to choose from. Here are several examples:

CAREERS FOR TECH GIRLS IN GRAPHIC DESIGN

To see what other graphic designers are doing, look at some graphic design blogs. These blogs can be a great way to learn and get inspired.

AisleOne: A blog about design, typography, minimalism, and modernism
Design Week: A UK design magazine
FormFiftyFive: An international showcase of design work
Friends of Type: The focus of this blog is on typographic design and lettering
Mirador: A graphic design studio in Paris
Typewolf: A blog about what's trending in type

GRAPHIC DESIGN WRAP-UP

"SHE OPENED DOORS": MURIEL COOPER

Muriel Cooper (1925–1994) began her career in print design and was successful as a designer. She then became one of the first graphic designers to shift her work to a computer. In 1967 Cooper took her first computer class at MIT. Although she was baffled by the class, she was able to understand that the computer held great potential for use in creating designs. At this point, her career took a turn toward the technological and she began to use her skills in digital design. Cooper became a cofounder of the Visible Language Workshop, a research group established in 1975, and she ran it until her death in 1994. This group would become part of MIT's famous Media Lab. Cooper did not write the computer code. However, she did apply her creative skills, working as the designer and thinker for the group. She was a teacher and had great influence on other designers. "She opened doors to let designers into rooms filled with programmers, mathematicians and computer scientists," said cofounder of the IDEO design group, Bill Moggridge, according to an article in the *New York Times*. "She showed that information screens filled with cryptic code could be filled with elegant typography, luscious colors and lively animations."

STUDY OTHER DESIGNERS

So what can you do while you're still in school and thinking about that graphic design career ... some day? There's plenty to do. The internet can

CAREERS FOR TECH GIRLS IN GRAPHIC DESIGN

Don't be afraid to show your graphic design work to family and friends. They can be a great support as you learn and grow your skills.

be a treasure trove for learning more about graphic design. Lots of graphic designers share their work on social media channels and platforms like Behance, Pinterest, and Tumblr, so you can look and learn. As you gain more practice and confidence, use these platforms to share your own work. These platforms offer an easy way to get your ideas and work out in the world where people can see them. They also provide a way for you to exchange ideas with other designers and get their feedback on your work.

Adriana Gascoigne, the founder and CEO of Girls in Tech, was asked what advice she might give today to her college self. Gascoigne said, in an interview at Women@Forbes, "Be fearless and just do it. If you're just sitting there and contemplating, things will never move forward. The world is so fast-paced now that there is no time to sit and think for too long. Don't think about the pros and cons too much—if you have an idea that you can't get out of your head, just go for it! I'm sure your family and friends will support you too, once they see the spark that your project lights in you. Always try and always ask—because if you don't, you'll never know. If you try and it's a no, then so be it. You won't lose anything. But if it's a yes? You'll open the door to infinite possibilities."

So when it comes to deciding on and chasing after the career that's right for you, sometimes you just have to "be fearless and just do it." If both the creative and the technical catch your eye, take a hard look at a graphic design career. Look and learn to see what is happening with design in the world all around you. Then get busy creating designs flowing from the fresh ideas of your own imagination.

Glossary

ADVERTISING AGENCY A business that plans, makes, and manages advertising for its clients. It is sometimes called a creative agency.

ANIMATOR A person who creates animated films.

COMPUTER-GENERATED IMAGERY (CGI) Digital graphics (computer graphics) used for the special effects that appear in movies, video games, or television.

CSS Stands for Cascading Style Sheets. A language used with HTML to define the layout of the HTML documents, covering things such as fonts, colors, background images, and margins.

DIGITAL CAMERA A camera that takes photos like a regular camera but records and stores the images in digital format (as data).

DIGITAL PORTFOLIO A computer-based collection of a person's work that is saved to a disk, a webpage, or a CD. It is a way for designers to showcase examples of their best work. (Sometimes called an electronic portfolio, online portfolio, or e-portfolio.)

DRAFTING TABLE Also called a drawing table. It is a table or desk where the table top can be flat or slanted and moved to different positions.

FREELANCER A self-employed person who usually works for multiple clients, instead of working for one employer for a regular salary.

GLOSSARY

GRAPHIC DESIGN SOFTWARE A software program (sometimes a collection of programs) that allows the user to create and edit computer graphics.

HTML Stands for hypertext markup language, a kind of code that is used to make documents on the web. It gives structure to the web content. The code is "hidden" when people view the finished product on the computer screen.

JAVASCRIPT A programming language that web developers use. Sometimes abbreviated as JS.

MEDIUM In graphic design or art, medium refers to the materials or substances used to create a design or a piece of art. (Plural form of the work is media or mediums.)

MULTIMEDIA Various forms of media used together to communicate with an audience. Examples might include text, sound, and animation used together or video and sound used together.

PORTFOLIO A collection of a person's work that showcases their skills. It is often used when a designer is applying to either a design school program or a job.

STAFF DESIGNER A person who works for a business handing any in-house graphic design needs the business might have.

STOP-MOTION ANIMATION A camera technique where the camera is stopped and started, one frame at

CAREERS FOR TECH GIRLS IN GRAPHIC DESIGN

a time, and the objects being photographed are moved slightly each time the camera is stopped so that when the images are replayed it appears that the objects are moving.

STORYBOARD A step-by-step sequence of drawings that display how a movie, animation, or game might appear in final form.

TYPOGRAPHY The arrangement of words, letters, symbols, and numbers on a page.

WEB DESIGNER A person who handles the design part of the work of creating a website.

WEB DEVELOPER A person who handles the coding part of the work of creating a website.

For More Information

American Institute of Graphic Arts (AIGA)
AIGA National Design Center
233 Broadway, Suite 1740
New York, NY 10279
(212) 807-1990
Website: http://www.aiga.org
Facebook, Instagram, and Twitter: @AIGAdesign
AIGA is the oldest and largest professional organization for graphic designers. They welcome student members and encourage student groups on college and university campuses.

Association of Registered Graphic Designers (RGD)
96 Spadina Avenue, Suite 210
Toronto, ON M5V 2J6
Canada
(888) 274-3668
Toronto: (416) 367-8819
Website: https://www.rgd.ca
Facebook and Pinterest: @RGDhub
Instagram and Twitter: @RGD
RGD offers Canadian designers a strong, supportive community where design is valued.

Graphic Artists Guild
31 West 34th Street, 8th floor
New York, NY 10001
(212) 791-3400
Website: https://www.graphicartistsguild.org
Facebook: @graphicartistsguild

Instagram: @graphic_artists_guild
Twitter: @gaguild
This association is focused on graphic artists, illustrators, web designers, and other creative careers. It provides education and job support for these creative professionals.

Graphic Designers of Canada (GDC)
Arts Court, 2 Daly Avenue
Ottawa, ON K1N 6E2
Canada
(877) 496-4453
Website: https://www.gdc.net
Facebook and Twitter: @GDCNational
GDC is a Canadian nonprofit that provides national certification for graphic and communication design.

Graphic Design USA (GDUSA)
89 Fifth Avenue, Suite 901
New York, New York 10003
(212) 696-4380
Website: http://gdusa.com
Facebook, Instagram, and Twitter: @gdusa
GDUSA is an information source for graphic design professionals. It offers a monthly e-newsletter.

National Association of Schools of Art and Design (NASAD)
11250 Roger Bacon Drive, Suite 21

FOR MORE INFORMATION

Reston, VA 20190
(703) 437-0700
Website: https://nasad.arts-accredit.org
NASAD is an organization of schools, conservatories, colleges, and universities that teach art and design. They set national standards for undergraduate and graduate degrees in art, design, and other related majors.

Society for News Design (SND)
424 E. Central Boulevard, Suite 406
Orlando, FL 32801
(407) 420-7748
Website: https://www.snd.org
Facebook: @societyfornewsdesign
Twitter: @SND
SND focuses on designers who create print, web, and mobile publications and products (visual journalism) by educating and promoting them as they work.

For Further Reading

Anderson, Denise. *Stand Out: Design a Personal Brand. Build a Killer Portfolio. Find a Great Design Job*. San Francisco, CA: Peachpit Press-Pearson Education, 2015.

Bierut, Michael. *How to Use Graphic Design to Sell Things, Explain Things, Make Things Look Better, Make People Laugh, Make People Cry, and (Every Once in a While) Change the World*. New York, NY: Harper Design, 2015.

Christen, Carol, and Richard N. Bolles. *What Color Is Your Parachute? For Teens* (Discover Yourself, Design Your Future, and Plan for Your Dream Job). Emeryville, CA: Ten Speed Press, 2015.

Clifford, John. *Graphic Icons: Visionaries Who Shaped Modern Graphic Design*. Atlanta, GA: Peachtree Press, 2014.

Greek, Joe. *A Career in Computer Graphics and Design* (Essential Careers). New York, NY: Rosen Publishing, 2015.

Hand, Carol. *Getting Paid to Produce Videos* (Turning Your Tech Hobbies into a Career). New York, NY: Rosen Publishing, 2017.

Heitkamp, Kristina Lyn. *Getting Paid to Make Games and Apps* (Turning Your Tech Hobbies into a Career). New York, NY: Rosen Publishing, 2017.

Heller, Steven, and Veronique Vienne. *Becoming a Graphic and Digital Designer: A Guide to Careers in Design*. Hoboken, NJ: John Wiley & Sons, Inc., 2015.

FOR FURTHER READING

Kleon, Austin. *Show Your Work!* New York, NY: Workman Publishing Co., Inc. 2014.

La Bella, Laura. *Careers for Tech Girls in Video Game Development* (Tech Girls). New York, NY: Rosen Publishing, 2016.

Niver, Heather Moore. *Women and Networking: Leveraging the Sisterhood.* New York, NY: Rosen Publishing, 2012.

Suen, Anastasia. *Internship & Volunteer Opportunities for People Who Love All Things Digital* (A Foot in the Door). New York, NY: Rosen Publishing, 2012.

Bibliography

Almosara, Janelle. "Becca Clason: Food for Thought." Design Made Happy, March 7, 2016. http://designmadehappy.com/2016/03/behind-the-scenes-with-becca-clason.

Au, Natalie. "The Best Advice 11 Inspiring Women in Tech Would Give to Their College Selves." Women@Forbes, December 29, 2016. https://www.forbes.com/sites/break-the-future/2016/12/29/the-best-advice-these-inspiring-women-in-tech-would-give-to-their-college-selves/#2e5a1e356b26.

Azzarello, Nina. "Interview with Jessica Walsh, Partner at Sagmeister & Walsh." Designboom, January 7, 2016. https://www.designboom.com/design/interview-jessica-walsh-sagmeister-walsh-graphic-design-01-07-2015.

Bureau of Labor Statistics. "Occupational Outlook Handbook: Film and Video Editors and Camera Operators." Retrieved September 30, 2017. https://www.bls.gov/ooh/media-and-communication/film-and-video-editors-and-camera-operators.htm.

Bureau of Labor Statistics. "Occupational Outlook Handbook: Graphic Designers." Retrieved September 30, 2017. https://www.bls.gov/ooh/arts-and-design/graphic-designers.htm#tab-1.

Bureau of Labor Statistics. "Occupational Outlook Handbook: Multimedia Artists and Animators." Retrieved September 30, 2017. https://www.bls.gov/ooh/arts-and-design/multimedia-artists-and-animators.htm#tab-1.

BIBLIOGRAPHY

Bureau of Labor Statistics. "Occupational Outlook Handbook: Photographers." Retrieved September 30, 2017. https://www.bls.gov/ooh/media-and-communication/photographers.htm#tab-1.

Carney, Rob. "12 Tools Every Graphic Designer Should Have in 2017." Creative Bloq, September 30, 2017. http://www.creativebloq.com/graphic-design/tools-every-graphic-designer-should-have-6133208/2.

Cezzar, Juliette. "What is Graphic Design?" American Institute of Graphic Arts, August 15, 2015. http://www.aiga.org/guide-whatisgraphicdesign.

Clason, Becca. "Becca Clason: About." Becca Clason. Retrieved August 23, 2017. http://www.beccaclason.com/ABOUT.

Clifford, John. "Visionaries Who Shaped Modern Graphic Design: Cipe Pineles." Peachpit, October 21, 2013. http://www.peachpit.com/articles/article.aspx?p=2140092.

Graphic Design Degree Hub. "What Types of Companies Hire Graphic Designers?" Retrieved September 30, 2017. http://www.graphicdesigndegreehub.com/faq/what-types-of-companies-hire-graphic-designers.

Graphic Design USA. "Gail Anderson To Creative Director at SVA Inhouse Studio." Retrieved September 30, 2017. http://gdusa.com/news/gail-anderson-to-creative-director-at-sva-inhouse-studio.

Heller, Steven. "Gail Anderson." American Institute of Graphic Arts, March 1, 2008. http://www.aiga.org/medalist-gailanderson.

History of Graphic Design. "The Age of Information: Postmodern Design: Paula Scher." Retrieved August 22, 2017. http://www.historygraphicdesign.com/the-age-of-information/postmodern-design/207-paula-scher.

Interview with Allison Blaylock, NC public school teacher and graphic designer. Charlotte, North Carolina. September 14, 2017.

Melanie. "Badass Lady Creatives [in History]: Cipe Pineles." Design Work Life, January 22, 2014. http://www.designworklife.com/2014/01/22/cipe-pineles.

National Association of Schools of Art & Design. "Students and Parents (FAQs)." Retrieved September 30, 2017. https://nasad.arts-accredit.org/students-parents.

National Association of Schools of Art & Design. "Welcome to NASAD." Retrieved August 25, 2017. https://nasad.arts-accredit.org.

Pentagram. "Paula Scher." Retrieved August 22, 2017. https://www.pentagram.com/about/paula-scher.

Pratt Institute. "Freshman and Transfer Portfolio Requirements." Retrieved September 30, 2017. https://www.pratt.edu/admissions/applying/applying-undergraduate/ug-application

BIBLIOGRAPHY

-requirements/freshman-and-transfer-portfolio-requirements.

Rawsthorn, Alice. "Muriel Cooper: The Unsung Heroine of On-screen Style." *New York Times*, September 30, 2007. http://www.nytimes.com/2007/09/28/style/28iht-design1.1.7670693.html?mcubz=0.

Robalino, Stephanie. "17 Female Designers to Watch in 2017." Hard Refresh, October 4, 2017. https://skillcrush.com/2017/02/13/women-designers-2017.

Sagmeister & Walsh. "About: Jessica Walsh." Retrieved September 30, 2017 http://sagmeisterwalsh.com/about/team.

Scotford, Martha. "Cipe Pineles." American Institute of Graphic Arts. Retrieved September 30, 2017. http://www.aiga.org/medalist-cipepineles.

Index

A

Adobe Creative Suite/Cloud, 30
Adobe MAX: The Creativity Conference, 53
advertising, 4, 5, 6, 19, 22, 36, 59
AIGA
  Design Conference, 53
  Medal, 9, 10, 18
AisleOne, 60
American Graphics Institute Summer Program, 15
American Institute of Graphic Arts, 7
Anderson, Gail, 9–10
Anderson Newton Design, 10
animation, 4, 8, 24–25, 27, 29, 31, 32, 59, 61
Appalachian State University, 47
apprenticeship, 48
art director, 5, 10, 16, 18, 20, 36, 44

B

Behance, 51, 62
Blaylock, Allison, 47
Boston Globe Sunday Magazine, 10
Bureau of Labor Statistics (BLS), 6, 10, 11, 21, 27, 31

C

Carbonmade, 51
CBS Records, 18
Charm magazine, 44
Chicago Design Museum (ChiDM), 39
Clason, Becca, 4–5
Clean Design, 55
commercial art, 10
communication design, 7
computer-generated imagery (CGI), 24–25
computer programming, 12, 13–14, 32, 40
computer programming languages, 33, 40–41
Cooper-Hewitt National Design Museum, 18
Cooper, Muriel, 61
Cooper Union, 18
Corel Paintshop, 43
cover letter, writing a, 53–54
creative director, 20
Crevado, 51
CSS, 33, 40
CyberLink PhotoDirector, 43

D

Design Made Happy, 5
Design Exchange (DX), 38
Design Week, 60
digital design art, 38–39

INDEX

Digital Media Academy, 13, 31
Dreamweaver, 41

E

Emagination Computer Camps, 13
entertainment industry, 27
ergonomics, 28–29

F

Ferrante, Janice, 55
Forbes magazine, 36
FormFiftyFive, 60
freelance work, 5–6, 20–22, 27, 36, 37–38, 59
Friends of Type, 60

G

Gascoigne, Adriana, 63
GIMP, 41
Girls in Tech, 63
Glamour magazine, 44
graphic design/designers
　advantages of a career in, 58–59
　alternate names for, 22
　associate's degree vs. bachelor's degree in, 22–23
　blogs, 59–60
　camps for, 13–15
　conferences, 52–53
　definition, 7–10
　finding schools for, 21, 22–23
　flexibility of a career as, 59
　high school courses for, 12–13
　job description, 16–19
　online courses for, 31–32
　projected job growth in, 6
　required skills for, 11
　requirements for a job in, 11–12
　where to work as, 19–22
　women owned companies for, 55

H

HOW Design Live, 53
HTML, 33, 36, 40

I

IDEO, 61
iD Tech Camps, 13
Illustrator, 31, 41
Inkscape, 41
internships, 11, 48, 49, 55

J

JavaScript, 33, 40
job interviews
　being prepared, 57
　first impressions, 56
　saying thanks, 57

77

K

KTD Creative, 55

L

lettering, 4, 60

M

Marquis Design, 55
Media Lab, 61
Metropolitan Opera, 18
Microsoft, 18
Mirador, 60
Moggridge, Bill, 61
Morpholio, 51
multimedia design/designers
  associate's degree vs. bachelor's degree in, 29–31
  median salary of, 27
  projected job growth for, 31
  what they do, 24–27
  where to work as, 27–29
Museum of Design Atlanta (MODA), 39
Museum of Modern Art (MoMA), 18, 36, 38

N

National Association of Schools of Art and Design (NASAD), 21
networking, 54–55
New York Art Directors Club, 44
New York City Ballet, 18
New York Film Academy, 13

O

Oberg, Debbie, 55
Oblique Design, 55
Otis College of Art and Design, 15
"Outstanding Main Title Design" Emmy, 25

P

Parsons School of Art and Design, 44
Pentagram, 17
Perkins, Natalie, 55
Perkins, Pam, 55
photography
  and design work, 45–46
  skills, 46–48
  tools, 42–43
photojournalism, 46
Photoshop, 31, 41, 43
Pineles, Cipe, 43–44
Pinterest, 62
portfolio, 11, 20, 41, 44, 57
  building a digital, 49–51
Pratt Institute, 49
Public Theater, 18

R

résumé, writing a, 51–54
Rolling Stone, 10

INDEX

S

Sagmeister & Walsh, 36
San Francisco Museum of Modern Art (SFMOMA), 38
Serif PhotoPlus, 43
Seventeen magazine, 44
Scher, Paula, 17–18
School of Visual Arts, 10, 18
SpotCo, 10
Squarespace, 51
stock photos, 46
storyboards, 25–27
Syracuse University Summer College for High School Students, 14

T

Tallent, Kate, 55
Tall Girl Design, 55
TechRocket, 32
Tumblr, 62
Tyler School of Art, 18
Type Directors Club Medal, 18
Typewolf, 60
typography, 10, 33, 60, 61

U

UCLA Department of Design Media Arts, 15

V

Vail, Julie, 55
Viewbook, 51
Victoria and Albert (V&A) Museum, 38
Visible Language Workshop, 61
Visual Arts Press, 10

W

Walsh, Jessica, 36
Watkins College of Art, Design, and Film Pre-College, 14
web design/designers,
  education requirements, 39–40
  skill requirements, 40–41
  specializations in, 40
  what they do, 33–35
  where they work, 35–38
web developer, 10, 35
Women@Forbes, 63
Willoughby, Ann, 55
Willoughby Design, 55

Y

Yale University, 18
Youth Digital, 32

ABOUT THE AUTHOR

Donna B. McKinney is a writer who lives in North Carolina. She spent many years writing about science and technology topics at the US Naval Research Laboratory in Washington, DC. Now she enjoys writing about science and technology for children and young adults. She is also a contributing writer for *Diversity in Action* magazine, where she writes about STEM careers.

PHOTO CREDITS

Cover wavebreakmedia/Shutterstock.com; cover, interior pages (circuit board illustration) © iStockphoto.com/Vladgrin; pp. 5, 34, 60 Rawpixel/Shutterstock.com; p. 8 Sean Pavone/Shutterstock.com; p. 9 Irina Lee/Wikimedia Commons/File: Louise Fili and Gail Anderson (cropped).jpg/CC BY 2.0; p. 14 Bill Freeman/Alamy Stock Photo; p. 17 Rob Watkins/Alamy Stock Photo; p. 20 PeopleImages/DigitalVision/Getty Images; p. 23 asiseeit/E+/Getty Images; p. 26 Mila Basenko/Shutterstock.com; p. 28 The Washington Post/Getty Images; p. 30 Maxim Apryatin/Shutterstock.com; p. 37 izusek/E+/Getty Images; p. 39 RosaIreneBetancourt 5/Alamy Stock Photo; p. 40 iinspiration/Shutterstock.com; p. 44 CBS Photo Archive/CBS/Getty Images; p. 45 Arctic-Images/Taxi/Getty Images; p. 50 Courtesy of Brian Garvey; p. 52 Denis Poroy/AP Images for Adobe; p. 56 Klaus Vedfelt/Riser/Getty Images; p. 62 Todd Warnock/DigitalVision/Getty Images.

Design and Layout: Nicole Russo-Duca; Editor: Rachel Aimee; Photo Researcher: Karen Huang